D0844874

FILM

Technology • People • Process

SARAH JONES

A+
Smart Apple Media

Media Wise series

Advertising   Film   Internet   Newspapers & Magazines

Produced for Hodder Wayland by Discovery Books Limited
Unit 3, 37 Watling Street, Leintwardine, Shropshire SY7 0LW, England

Editor: Patience Coster, Series editor: Victoria Brooker, Series design: Mind's Eye Design,
Commissioned Photographs: Marysia Lachowicz

Published in the United States by Smart Apple Media
1980 Lookout Drive, North Mankato, Minnesota 56003

Library of Congress Cataloging-in-Publication Data

Jones, Sarah.
Film / by Sarah Jones.
p. cm. — (Media wise)
Summary: Describes film production from idea to final product, and profiles various jobs in
film, including scriptwriter, producer, composer, and stills photographer.
Includes bibliographical references and index.
ISBN 1-58340-256-X
1. Motion pictures—Vocational guidance—Juvenile literature. [1.Motion pictures—Vocational
guidance. 2. Vocational guidance.] I. Title. II. Series.

PN 1995.9.P75 J63 2003
791.43'0293—dc21   2002191173

9 8 7 6 5 4 3 2 1

Picture acknowledgments: Channel 4 Films 9; Columbia Pictures 26; Corbis 11 (Rufus F.
Folkks), 15 (Robert Maass), 16 (Hulton-Deutsch Collection), 30, 37 (Tim Wright), 39 (Dean
Conger), 44 (Horace Bristol), 48 (Hulton-Deutsch Collection), 50 (Owen Franken), 55 (Angelo
Hornak), 58 (Kevin Fleming), 59 (Catherine Karnow); Dreamworks 5; EON 18, 19; Ronald
Grant Archive 4, 22, 35, 47; House and Moorhouse 10; Impact Photos 56 (Giles Barnard);
Magnolia Productions 12; MGM 17; Paramount Pictures 27; Pathe 25; Popperfoto 52;
Popperfoto/Reuter 32, 51; Silver Productions 21; Touchstone 6; 20th Century Fox 7, 34, 36;
20th Century Fox/Paramount 24; UIP/Dreamworks 8; Warner Bros 13, 23.

Cover: Corbis (Tim Wright)

CONTENTS

What Is Film? 4

From Idea to Finance 6

The Production Team 16

The Shoot 30

Post-Production 44

The Journey to the Theater 50

Getting a Job in the Industry 56

Glossary 60

Useful Addresses 62

Books to Read 63

Index 64

WHAT IS FILM?

There are many different types of film. The three most common types are feature, documentary, and animation (or a combination of these resulting in, for example, the "docu-drama" film). A feature is a fictional film, usually between 90 and 130 minutes long, that is shown in commercial theaters. A documentary, or nonfiction film, is any film that has as its subject real-life persons, events, or situations. Animation describes any film that gives life to drawings, models, cut-outs, or computer image representations of people, objects, and animals by filming and projecting them at a speed to give them a sense of movement.

Commercial or independent?

Another distinction is between commercial and independent films. Commercial films are made primarily for profit and entertainment, often by a Hollywood studio. Independent films are made by much smaller companies often set up simply for the purpose of making the film. They tend to concentrate on artistic, symbolic, or educational qualities rather than on making a profit. In this book, we are going to look at the various stages involved in the making of a feature film. However, many of the stages are also relevant for documentary and animated films, and all stages apply to commercial or independent ventures.

The early days of movies—filmmakers setting up a shot in Hollywood in 1922.

The process of making a feature film is long and complicated. It may involve hundreds of people, lots of specialized equipment, and—sometimes—millions of dollars.

Where did it all start?

Motion picture photography was invented in Europe towards the end of the 19th century. By the beginning of the 20th century, silent moving pictures (often with live piano accompaniment) were being used to tell stories to assembled crowds. It was in the United States that the medium of cinema was to flourish most spectacularly. By 1910, American filmmakers had begun to realize the potential of California for location filming. Its clear, dry weather and variety of landscapes were especially good for the Western movies that proved so popular at the time. Before long, a small town called Hollywood was overrun with film studios, and its name came to stand for the industry as a whole.

By 1912, the craze for movie-making had developed into a significant and long-lasting trend. Films dominated the first half of the 20th century as the most important means of mass entertainment and, against all expectations, they managed to survive the advent of television in the 1950s. Today most countries have their own distinctive film industries, and film production has become an entirely international business.

The making of modern animated films such as Antz, *above, may seem complicated, but it has its roots in some of the earliest movies. In 1902, French film director George Méliès experimented with animation in his short film,* A Trip to the Moon.

Media Fact

The first documentary

Although "slice of life" moving images were popular from the start of movies, the first full-length documentary film was not made until 1922. Called *Nanook of the North*, it was a study of Inuit life in northern Canada.

FROM IDEA
TO FINANCE

The first stage in the life of a film is the idea. The writer, director, or producer of the film may provide the idea in the form of a book or a play, or there may be an original idea for the script, often inspired by a true event. An original script is not based on a previously produced or published work, but is written directly for the screen. An adapted script is based on source material already in existence, such as a novel.

The script (also known as the screenplay) is a written description of the film. It includes details about the characters, their actions and relations to one another, information about costumes, props, and sets, and instructions to camera, sound, and other technical crews. The script is written months or even years before the film is released and is used by the cast and crew as a blueprint for the finished film.

Pretty Woman *is an example of a popular romantic comedy film that was not adapted from a book or play, but based on an original script.*

The pitch

The next step is for the producer to raise the money that is needed to make the film, or at least to get it started. The producer puts together a plan (package) and presents (pitches) it to potential investors. These may range from government agencies, who are often eager to support the national film industry, to private individuals who are interested in making money from the film industry. In Hollywood, the pitch is handled by a studio executive, and, since millions of dollars may be involved, it is treated as seriously as any big business deal.

The credits at the end of a film give an idea of how expensive it was to produce. A typical big-budget movie employs up to 700 people, from set builders to make-up artists. Transportation, accommodation, catering, set rental, and insurance are all additional costs, as are the costs of editing equipment, sound mix facilities, and producing the master and copies of the film. The money that is spent before shooting starts is called the "above-the-line" cost. This includes the fees for the producer, writer, director, leading actors, and other key personnel who contribute to the creative vision of the film. Above-the-line costs tend to be fixed fees and therefore should not change during the production process.

Shakespeare's plays are full of visual ideas and have been adapted for the cinema many times. One of the most successful recent adaptations was Romeo and Juliet *in 1997.*

"Below-the-line" costs include on-set and post-production expenses, and all other expenditures for cast and crew, equipment, film stock, costumes, props, transportation, and facilities. These costs are not fixed, because filming is unpredictable and more may need to be spent in some areas than others. For example, if bad weather delays the shoot, or a new location has to be found and the script rewritten, these things will add to the below-the-line costs. The producer must find the money for this from another part of the budget, renegotiate the deal with the investors, or find new money elsewhere. Ideally, the contingency (emergency) portion of the budget will cover some of the unplanned costs.

Gladiator, *directed by Ridley Scott and starring Russell Crowe, cost an enormous amount of money to make. The investment paid off, as its strong story, powerful performances, and impressive special effects ensured it was a success at the box office and at the 2001 Academy Awards (Oscars).*

To give an idea of the total amount of money needed to make a film, the blockbuster *Gladiator* cost almost $100 million to make, while the surprise hit *Trainspotting* cost $3 million. It is calculated that a film becomes profitable once it has made two and a half times its total cost at the box office and on other pre-sales (to television, video, and DVD). The money that is made after production, marketing, and distribution costs have been taken into account is the film's profit.

In the first instance, money is needed to pay the writer to put the initial ideas onto paper or to begin to adapt the source material for the screen (script development). A Hollywood studio, such as Warner Brothers, Paramount, or Columbia Tristar, would already have the finances to support this stage, provided that the studio executive is convinced by the writer and writer's agent that the idea is likely to make a profit.

Films produced in the independent sector rarely have this kind of advance backing. The main task of the producer here is to persuade banks, investment companies, and wealthy individuals that it is a good idea to sink money into the film's development and production.

The treatment

Initially, an outline (a brief summary of the plot) and treatment (an early, abbreviated script) of up to 25 pages are presented to the investors. The outline and treatment include a detailed storyline and suggestions for cast and locations. If the director or producer already has a good reputation in the industry, the initial idea alone might be sufficient to sell the film.

Media Fact

The studio system

In 1912, the major U.S. production companies formed a "studio system." Their goal was to set up facilities for the fast, cheap, mass production of feature films to satisfy the enormous demand for movies around the world, and to control distribution and exhibition. The main crew and stars were employed on long-term contracts to guarantee their loyalty and help create a recognizable "house style." Each studio developed its own special brand of films, building on successful stories, popular stars, and reusable sets and costumes. Central to the working of this new "factory-style" arrangement was the producer, who wielded formidable power. Although the studio system restricted creative freedom, it produced some classic productions and became the basis of American filmmaking for much of the 20th century.

Trainspotting, *directed by Danny Boyle and starring Ewan McGregor, was a major British hit, despite its controversial story based on drug culture and its very low budget compared to Hollywood films.*

Muriel's Wedding

P. J. Hogan, the director of the Australian film *Muriel's Wedding*, wrote a detailed 30-page treatment of his first film and sent it to the Australian Film Commission, asking for A$5,000 to fund script development. They rejected it outright, telling him it was terrible and should never be made. Eventually he acquired some money from a smaller funding body and wrote the script in three months. The film took two years to make. When released, it won awards for best film, best actress, and best supporting actress from the Australian Film Institute.

If a film distributor has already shown interest in the project, it is important to include details of these discussions, especially if there is a particular target audience in mind, or if any marketing initiatives have been considered. The investors will ask questions about the potential for additional money-making activities, such as merchandising and partnerships that maximize public awareness of the film. For example, the producers of *Independence Day* teamed up with Burger King to market a whole range of special offers, merchandise, and promotions that benefited both the film and the food chain. The investor will also expect the producer to have considered the possibility of increasing profit through video, DVD, and television sales. Even if the package is strong, original, and exciting, there is no guarantee that the film will make a profit since most of the ideas about income are based on guesswork. But a well thought-out package helps to gain the confidence of the investors and shows that the producer knows the business, has considered every aspect carefully, and is serious about spending the investors' money wisely.

The deal

The business agreement between the producer and the investors is called the "deal." The terms of the deal vary according to the type of film proposed and its potential income. It is rare for a film to have a single financial backer; often an independent production has a range of investors from several different countries, and one of the producer's jobs is to manage the interests and demands of each of these. It sometimes takes months or years for different investments to come together at the right time. Film festivals such as Cannes and the American Film Market are vital for independent producers or directors trying to sell their packages to potential backers, or for those with films already made who are looking for a distribution deal.

The Cannes Film Festival, held in the south of France each May, is the most prestigious and glamorous independent film festival in the world. Many a hopeful producer or film director will try to strike a deal there.

However, the fact that a deal has been struck does not indicate that thereafter the making of the film will be smooth sailing. Some ideas are funded for script development but are developed no further than that. In other cases, the production might go ahead, but the film is never released because of lack of confidence from the investors and a reluctance on their part to spend more money on an expensive marketing campaign. Films such as this might be released directly to video or television so that they still have a chance of recouping at least a part of the initial investment.

Many successful directors, such as Woody Allen (on set, above left), also write their own scripts.

Writing the script

Once the outline and treatment have been approved, the next stage is the writing of a full treatment, or first draft, of the script. This is submitted to the investors with a proposed budget and a storyboard (a series of drawings, cartoon style, which shows how the script could be shot) of some key scenes. The producers also submit the professional credentials of the main crew members (director, composer, cinematographer) and any stars who have shown positive interest or are secured, and a draft working schedule for the production to show how long it will take to make the film.

Once financial backing has been secured for the project, it is discussed by the creative team. The full script is written and rewritten many times, beginning with the development of characters, dialogue, and plot. Each draft (version) of the script is commented on by all involved, especially by the financial backers, who will want to see a return on their often huge investments. Weaker scenes may be dropped, new characters brought in, dialogue improved, and more action added.

The film's writer carries out most of the research required to produce a coherent script. But the script's development also usually involves many meetings between the writer, producer, director, and other key personnel. More often than not, and especially in Hollywood, the writer is seen as the least important member of the creative team, despite having created the foundation for the film! There have been many unfortunate occasions in which writer and director have disagreed on the script's development, and the writer, not the director, has been unceremoniously removed from the project.

The scriptwriter often talks through the script with the main actors to explain where certain ideas have come from. This process helps the actors to develop the characters fully. Here scriptwriter Robert Towne (right) discusses a scene with actor Mel Gibson.

Script doctors

A script editor is often employed to help out with rewrites or to work during production on redrafts if the original writer has been removed or is busy elsewhere. In extreme cases, a script doctor is hired: this is a highly paid professional screenwriter who is called in to "rescue" a script that is considered to be inadequate in some way. The script doctor is usually hired just as production is about to start, or even when shooting is underway. The script doctor's name may not appear in the final credits, but word of his or her help will usually get out.

The script may be rewritten up to 25 times before the shoot has ended. There may be

A script meeting is often held before rehearsals begin. It involves all the principal cast and crew, who read through the script and jot down what they need to prepare for each scene.

further artistic thoughts, the existing script may contain scenes that are impossible to shoot for technical reasons, or budget restraints may result in further redrafts taking place on set. Each script redraft is produced on a different color paper, so that everyone involved knows which is the latest version of the script.

The Scriptwriter

The scriptwriter provides the written outline, otherwise known as the script or screenplay, of a film. This contains the dialogue, descriptions of the main characters and settings, and some basic camera directions. One page of script represents about one minute of film, so a standard feature film needs about 90 to 120 pages of script.

The scriptwriter's job often begins long before pre-production starts. If a scriptwriter is working on a true story, then he or she needs to research the subject thoroughly. Many scriptwriters like to work closely with the director at this stage, as it is important to agree at the outset on the direction the film should take. Once an approach to the material is agreed upon, the scriptwriter begins to write. However, some scriptwriters prefer to work on the script independently and complete it before a director is attached to the project.

During production, the role that the scriptwriter plays depends on the director and the location. During a shoot, the director can become bogged down in details, so it may be useful to have someone there who can remember the overall shape of the film. Once the schedule is worked out, it often becomes clear that not all of the script will get filmed. The scriptwriter looks hard at the schedule and marks the scenes that are essential; he or she then says which

scenes are dispensable or can be modified. By altering the script slightly, the writer can save the production time and money. If a scene needs to be cut, the scriptwriter may add a line or two to another scene so that the story still holds together. The writer may also make suggestions during the editing process.

A scriptwriter's job may be lonely, but seeing his or her work come alive on screen usually makes it all worthwhile.

THE PRODUCTION TEAM

Once the film script is written and most of the money has been promised, pre-production work can begin. Pre-production involves (at least) the producer, director, assistants, and administrative staff, and may take from six months to two years to complete. The work entails scheduling—planning the time needed to shoot the script; budgeting—working out how best to make use of the money available; and casting—finding the right actors to bring the script to life. The technical team (crew) is assembled, locations or studios are identified, and insurance, accounting, and legal details are arranged. The cinematographer (also known as the director of photography or DOP) and director decide on which film stock or video format to use. If special effects are required, especially for action, adventure, science fiction, or horror movies, the details must be planned carefully.

A storyboard is prepared for a Hollywood film during the 1950s. Storyboards may be quick sketches or more elaborate drawings.

Usually the producer is responsible for the production costs and aspects of the planning, and the director is responsible for making artistic decisions. However, these two elements are inseparable, and the producer and director work very closely when making decisions about staff, casting, design, lighting, and locations. They need to have a good working relationship and to trust each other. As filmmaking is so expensive, the pre-production stage is vital for dealing in advance with any potential problems, preparing for the worst, and trying to ensure that the shooting schedule is kept to and that the process runs as smoothly as possible.

Storyboarding and scheduling

During pre-production, the script is broken down into separate scenes. The writer, director, and production designer create a full storyboard so that they can visualize how the film will progress. A storyboard is a series of drawings, similar to a comic strip, that represents every shot that will eventually make up the completed film. Today, storyboarding is often computer-generated. The ways in which storyboards are used varies according to the working methods of the director. Some directors use them to work out a particularly complicated scene in advance, such as an action scene in, for example, the *Mission Impossible* films.

Others, such as great British film director Alfred Hitchcock, might want to storyboard the whole film. In addition to drawings, storyboards also have captions that indicate dialogue cues and details of camera instructions.

A scene from North by Northwest, *directed by Alfred Hitchcock, who used meticulous storyboarding to map out all his films in advance.*

Detailed storyboards are produced for the James Bond films to ensure that the special effects and stunts are planned thoroughly. This storyboard is from the film Tomorrow Never Dies.

Ken Adam, the production designer on many of the early James Bond movies, such as *You Only Live Twice*, created the most amazingly intricate, colorful, and artistic storyboards to convey the overall visual concept of the film. These enabled him, with the art director, to bring the required amount of escapism and invention to the action scenes. Most storyboards, however, are like detailed sketches and are referred to, mainly by the director and DOP, throughout the shoot along with the most up-to-date version of the script.

Next the producer, director, production manager, and DOP prepare a shooting schedule. This involves working out the timetable and logistical plan of a production. It is vital to work out exactly what should happen in each scene, who and what will be needed, and for how long. Thorough preparation and planning during pre-production can save time and money during the production and post-production phases.

If the writer is still available at this stage, he or she can help to point out which scenes are most important to the story and which could be left out if necessary to cut costs. Everyone in production will have a copy of the final version of the script (the "shooting script"), which includes dialogue, action, scene descriptions, and camera instructions, although there are usually continual revisions throughout the shoot. It is the responsibility of the production manager or assistant to ensure that everyone has the corrected, current script (which is sometimes updated on a daily basis).

The storyboard and script are broken down by location and by "set-up" (each new camera

This scene from Tomorrow Never Dies *shows how accurate the storyboard was in this case.*

position) to create the shooting schedule. To save time and money, all scenes that take place on one set or location are usually filmed at the same time, even if this means filming the story out of sequence. The shoot is also restricted by when people and locations are available, and union regulations demand that the cast and crew need regular breaks. The producer and director will often work out a priority list of the shots they must get each day. This is followed by a secondary list of shots to get after that, followed by a luxury list if all goes so well that there is extra time to play with. A reasonable shooting ratio is 10 to 1; this means that 10 times as much film is shot as is used in the final film. On a good day's shoot, perhaps five minutes of usable film will be shot. If just one film unit (set of crew and equipment) is used, a full-length feature film may take up to six or seven weeks to shoot.

Budgeting

A rough budget is produced for the investors, and a certain amount of money is secured for production to continue. During pre-production, the producer and director fine-tune the budget and decide on spending priorities. The shooting schedule helps them to work out what is needed and for how long, and quotes are obtained for the rental of post-production facilities. At this stage, negotiating skills are very useful to bargain for the best prices for cast, crew, and equipment.

The budget of a film production is divided into above-the-line and below-the-line costs (discussed in chapter two). A production accountant is brought in to help put together the budget in detail and set up the systems to ensure that money is spent according to plan and records are kept.

The Producer

A producer's job is to gather together the right team of people and to challenge, support, and encourage all those whose efforts will bring the film to fruition. The producer is also ultimately responsible for managing the practical, financial, legal, contractual, and organizational aspects of production.

During pre-production, the producer ensures that the script is ready and supervises rewrites if necessary. He or she needs to be certain that the most suitable—and most talented—team is assembled, with the right attitude for the particular needs of the project. The producer negotiates fees with agents and works with the legal team on all the contracts (including those of employees, financing and distribution agreements, insurance policies, and so on). He or she communicates constantly with the financiers (who will want to be kept informed about, if not to approve, certain key elements of the team). The producer listens carefully to the needs arising from the preparation process, since all needs have financial implications. The producer must keep communication lines open so that he or she knows what is in the minds of the various members of the production team and must collaborate with, take care of, and encourage every team member.

On set, the producer ensures that the director and the team are working to their optimum capacity and keeping on schedule and on budget. Although the producer should take a flexible approach, he or she needs to look for the weak points in the production and strengthen them (or, if absolutely necessary, replace them). The producer also hosts visits from interested members of the press and arranges for publicity photographic shoots.

In post-production, a lot of the producer's time is spent on music clearances (negotiating and paying for the copyright on music used in the film that has not been specially composed and performed for it). With the accountant, the producer gathers the invoices, checks the budget, and tries to ensure that the costs are as originally anticipated. If crucial material needs to be re-shot, or a new sequence or new shots need to be added, the producer must ensure that more money is found to finance these. On the release of the film, it is the producer's job to enter it in festivals, organize test screenings, coordinate marketing, and have posters designed.

The producer visits the set on most days of the shoot to see how filming is going and to deal with any major problems.

Cast and crew

To a large extent, the success of a film may depend on the popularity of its stars. Producers and directors know that actors such as Johnny Depp, below, can pull in the crowds at the box office.

Casting on big-budget films is usually carried out via agents. The process of casting involves choosing performers to fill the roles in a film, and it is always an area of conflict and controversy. Standard auditions, or "screen tests," are still an important part of the process, but for major roles today, the stars are usually hired at a private meeting after they have read the script, and following lengthy negotiations regarding fees. The casting of commercial films is heavily influenced by how much money the star is likely to pull in at the box office, and is therefore dependent on his or her current popularity.

The director and producer are usually responsible for casting the leading roles of a mainstream film. Other roles tend to be negotiated by a casting director with the agent of a particular performer. Agents represent the interests of actors and crew members. They seek work for their clients through advertising and networking (developing useful contacts by attending parties and film premieres). Agents strike deals on financial terms and conditions in return for a percentage (usually around 10 percent) of their clients' earnings. An agent can be a powerful force in the film industry, especially if he or she represents a range of talented actors and crew.

The casting of child actors poses a particular challenge. It is usually done through schools, theaters, and television advertisements, as well as by specialist agents. Carefully worded contracts are drawn up, and a chaperone is hired to keep an eye on the younger actors.

Child stars such as Macaulay Culkin, below, need protection from the more cut-throat aspects of the film industry. But some child actors go on to become very shrewd businesspeople, too!

Legal contracts

Lawyers with specialist film industry knowledge are often used to help draw up specific contracts with a particular actor or crew member. Otherwise, standard contracts are used as written agreements between the production company and everyone involved in the making of a film. These help to protect both parties in the event of an argument or misunderstanding.

The film Titanic *cost more than $200 million to make and included some of the most daring camera movements and special effects seen to date.*

Equipment, facilities rental, and film stock

Quotes for equipment, facilities rental, and film stock are obtained at an early stage, as these are vital but expensive elements of the filmmaking process. Often an established DOP will provide some of his or her own equipment, but most will have to be rented from specialist companies. If the script breakdown and storyboarding process highlight a need for special equipment to create certain types of shots or special effects, these should be booked. It is the task of the producer and production manager to negotiate the best deals possible.

The director will also have decided at an earlier stage what sort of film stock he or she wants to use to make the film. The most common format for feature films is 35mm film, although digital formats are beginning to become popular because they are cheaper and require less equipment. *The Blair Witch Project*, made in 1999, was one of the first films to use digital formats during the production process. The filmmakers decided to have the actors themselves film part of the story with a digital camera to create a realistic and frightening atmosphere. Elsewhere, different formats, such as 16mm or Super-8mm film, are occasionally used in certain scenes to create a particular effect.

The film stock used in The Blair Witch Project *(above) was chosen to help create the effect of a low-budget, student film.*

Insurance

Special insurance coverage is needed to protect the production company in the event of an accident, damage, or loss during the making of the film, especially if special equipment or a foreign location is being used, or a dangerous stunt or large crowd scene is to be included. The most basic insurance package will add one and a half percent to the film's budget. At this stage, the producer needs to draw up a risk assessment—a list of all the things that could go wrong and the steps that will be taken to prevent those things from happening. If the film is being shot on location, the producer will often produce a risk assessment with the help of the location manager.

The rise of the feature film

Beginning in 1909, filmmakers started making films of more than one reel (10 to 20 minutes) in length. In the United States, these reels were released one a week to meet strict regulations set by the Motion Pictures Patent Company. These longer "features" were very popular and soon replaced the mixture of short films that up until then had been screened at nickelodeons (makeshift movie theaters).

Location scouting

This involves looking for the places outside the studio (interior) where a film is to be shot. Location scouting is particularly important if the film is to look as true-to-life as possible, even though the actual location will be transformed for production by the lighting and set design and props that are brought in. For most feature films, the location manager is mainly responsible for finding suitable locations according to the instructions of the producer and director.

The location manager first goes on a reconnaissance, or "recce," of likely locations and looks at all the possibilities before making any final decisions. The recce may be carried out

Filming on location often involves redecorating the facades of buildings and closing city streets to traffic.

The Production Designer

The production designer coordinates costumes, sets, makeup, etc., and, with the director, creates the overall look of the film. Firstly, the production designer produces drawings and plans showing the architecture and color schemes of the set. He or she is usually responsible for a production design unit, which handles the construction and painting of sets, or modifies locations so that they can be filmed.

Secondly, the production designer must ensure that all the required props are found and arranged on set as the director wants them. A costume designer works as part of the production design unit, planning and preparing the wardrobe for the production. The production designer often must work on very tight deadlines, as a building that is perfect for a scene may be available for only one day, or even for just a few hours. Sometimes, if the director needs to reshoot some scenes, another location must be made to look like the original one if the latter is no longer available. At this point, the production designer and the design unit have to work extra hard to ensure that it is impossible to tell the difference between the two!

The production designer (above right) refines ideas for sets and costumes according to any changes to the script.

Set dressers have to make sure that all props are in place before the cast arrives and filming starts.

via an agency that has been set up to promote a particular area to film producers as a way of bringing business into the community. The location manager also manages the smooth running of the location shoots, including obtaining the required permission to film, organizing the catering for cast and crew, keeping the property owners and neighbors happy, and ensuring that nothing is damaged or stolen and no one is injured. The location manager may also need to arrange for city streets to be sealed off from regular traffic for brief periods during filming.

Finally, the producer, production manager, and assistants work hard to organize the logistical details within the budget. These include transportation, catering, accommodations, and communication systems. The production team must ensure that the film shoot runs as smoothly and efficiently as possible.

The Production Assistant

The production assistant (PA) works closely with the producer, from the initial pitch to the final post-production and delivery. The PA may work on two or three projects at once, spending time on the studio floor ensuring that the shoot is going well, checking on cast arrangements and set construction for the next shoot, and then perhaps scheduling and "crewing-up" for another.

The production assistant also deals with everyday paperwork—invoices, timesheets, and filing —and attends various meetings. During post-production, the production assistant may work in the editing suite, but usually he or she remains in the office to sort out any problems that arise while the producer is away.

It takes persistence to become a PA, and the value of work experience should not be underestimated. It is important to learn how the film-making process works from beginning to end. This can only be done on the job—for example, by carrying cameras and batteries around muddy fields, taking detailed continuity notes, or searching through hundreds of videos for a piece of footage. Production assistants work long hours—14-hour work days are not uncommon.

The production assistant is involved in all stages of filming and sorts out administrative problems on a day-to-day basis.

THE SHOOT

When the shooting of the film takes place, the cast and crew come together after weeks, or sometimes months, of preparation. This is the most expensive period in the life of a film, with the cost of hiring hundreds of people and truckloads of equipment, not to mention the expense of hiring the studio. There are usually transportation and accommodation costs to cover as well. It is impossible to know in advance exactly what will happen during a film's shoot, as so many things can affect the schedule (bad weather is one of the most common problems).

Camera operators work with the DOP and director to ensure that filming is effective and efficient.

It is important to pick up the actors' dialogue clearly. In a group scene such as this, a boom operator is needed to hold the microphone.

Production is also the most exhausting part of the process, with everyone working around the clock to get the job done as well as they can in the shortest possible time. Actors must know their lines perfectly, caterers must have the right food prepared, all the necessary equipment needs to be in place and working, and so on. While each director has his or her own way of approaching the production stage, there are certain phases in the process that are common to all films. In this chapter we look at the most important activities that take place during production, all of which need to be carried out to achieve the best possible image and sound ready for post-production. The tasks described are the main jobs carried out by the crew—the team of technicians involved in the production stage of a film.

Media Fact

The star system

Around 1908, actors started serving longer contracts with certain studios. These actors' faces became familiar with mass film audiences, despite studio attempts to keep them anonymous so that they could not demand higher fees. In the early days of movies, films rarely included credits, so stars' names were invented by the press and the public. These made-up names were eventually used more and more by the studios to publicize the films. Eventually, stars with invented names such as Marilyn Monroe, Rock Hudson, and Humphrey Bogart became the stuff of movie legend.

The Director

The director is responsible for the end result of the film and needs to ensure that the cast and crew all understand the goals of the production.

The director acts as the vision and voice behind the film, sharing creative control with the producer. He or she works on the film through all the stages, from idea to completion, in consultation with the crew. During pre-production, the director works with the writer on getting the script to final draft stage. He or she will also choose the crew in consultation with the producer, concentrating first on the DOP, production, costume, and makeup designers, editor, sound mixer, and composer.

Casting the actors is important at this stage. The director works with the casting director on choices for each part and is involved in the final decision-making process of the casting session. The director and producer choose the locations and discuss the set plan, if one is needed for the script. The director works with the production manager to prepare the schedule and make sure all technical requirements have been considered. They discuss how each scene will be shot, consider the potential problems and possible solutions at each location, and rehearse with the actors.

On set, the main goal of the director is to achieve the best performances possible from the actors, and the best possible shots from the director of photography. By the end of the shoot, the team will have produced the raw material (the rushes) from which the final film is made. The director must constantly keep in mind how the scene will look when all the shots are edited together.

The director usually works out a routine for each scene. By "blocking" each scene—mapping out the ways actors will sit, stand, or move about, deciding where props and scenery will go, and working out camera movements—the director has a clear idea of what needs to be done. Then the actors go for final costume and makeup preparations while the technical crew sets the lights, gets the camera in position, and rigs for the sound. There is a last rehearsal with everyone, and then the director starts to shoot. The production team needs to complete the daily schedule as set, and within budget.

As soon as the director has finished shooting, he or she works with the editor on a "rough cut" of the film. The director then goes through various stages of cuts of the film and mixes of the sound, in consultation with the producer, until they reach an agreement on the "final cut." The director works with the composer and sound editor to agree on music, sound effects, and any extra dialogue, which are then mixed together to produce a final soundtrack. The director attends color-grading sessions (these involve adjusting the color and brightness of the film) with the DOP and discusses titles, credits, and publicity. Finally the whole film is completed for a preview screening and sometimes a test screening, after which it could get changed again!

"It is important to decide on and design the 'look' of the film as early as possible and discuss this with all main cast and crew. I also try to get to know the script and storyboard so well that I can play it through in my head."

"You are surrounded, hopefully, by a group of people who are as passionate and mad as you are! Every time you have a vision of it in your head, and always when you see the final product it falls short of this—but perhaps each time you get just a little bit closer."
Jean Stewart, director

The director uses a small lens to see how a scene will look on film.

Image

Apart from the director, probably the most important person on set is the director of photography, who is in charge of lighting the set and the actors, setting up and moving the camera, positioning the lights, selecting appropriate lenses, film stock, and color filters, and working out the composition of shots. In general, the DOP is the person who creates the visual identity of the film, along with the director and production designer. The DOP has a number of assistants. The main one is the focus puller, who is responsible for adjusting the focus of the camera lens during a shot.

The filming of special effects such as fires and explosions can be very dangerous, and great care has to be taken to ensure that no one is hurt.

The DOP also needs to work on producing any special effects required by the script. There are three types of effects: mechanical effects, such as simulated explosions, fires, floods, and storms; illusions created by "trick" photography; and digital effects created by computer graphics software during post-production.

During the shoot, the clapper loader is responsible for marking the beginning of each "take" (each run of film through the camera as it records a shot). The clapper loader does this by "clapping" the sticks on the clapperboard while holding it in front of the camera. Because image and sound are recorded separately, the sound of the clapperboard helps when matching them together during post-production.

The Director of Photography

The role of the director of photography is to create the "look" of the film through lighting, color, and the choice of camera angles and shots. Lighting is very important to the mood, style, and atmosphere of a film.

The DOP uses the pre-production period to get to know the script and director well. The director and DOP discuss ideas and look at paintings, photos, and other films; in this way, the DOP reaches an understanding of the director's vision. Sometimes the DOP goes on a technical "recce" with other key personnel to all the locations that are to be used in the film, and discusses how the scenes will be shot, taking photos as a record. The DOP then talks to the gaffer (chief electrician, or "spark") about how he or she wants to light each scene. The DOP also talks to the chief grip (whose team moves equipment, props, and cameras around) about any special equipment they might need. Such equipment might include a "crane" (a large trolley on top of which is mounted an extended arm for the camera) or a "dolly" (a mobile camera platform mounted on wheels that is used for tracking shots in which the camera moves along rails to follow the action smoothly). The DOP also attends scheduling meetings in which he or she is asked to estimate how long each scene will take to shoot.

On set, the DOP watches the actors rehearse and discusses with the director exactly how to shoot each scene, communicating any changes of plan to the rest of the team. The DOP tells the focus puller which lens to put on the camera, and the loader which film stock to load into the camera. The DOP becomes involved in post-production once the film has been "fine cut" or "locked off" —in other words, when the main cut and the soundtrack are brought together. Then he or she begins the grading process: this involves checking the color and asking for it to be made brighter, darker, warmer, or cooler if necessary. The grading process is a very important part of the final look of the film.

The DOP is responsible for making sure that each shot looks good and covers the action effectively.

The clapper loader's job may look simple, but it requires timing and precision.

The chief electrician on a film crew is called the gaffer. The gaffer answers to the DOP and supervises the work of a number of electricians. He or she looks after all major electrical installations on the set, including lighting and power. The gaffer's main assistant is known as the best boy—even though a man, or a woman, may do this job.

In addition, teams of manual laborers (grips) are also hired to carry out the heavy work under the leadership of the key grip. These on-set workers are often responsible for several different jobs, such as setting up equipment or scenery or laying tracks on which the cameras can move around. Large productions have a range of specialist grips who take responsibility for each set of equipment or scenery.

A good sound recordist is essential to the production process.

Sound

The sound recordist concentrates mainly on picking up the actors' dialogue as clearly as possible. The sound recordist must make sure that he or she tapes any sound effects that are unique to the location, such as water running or the noise of crowd scenes (the latter is difficult to recreate realistically in post-production). He or she also records "wild tracks"; this is sound recorded separately from the images and added at the editing stage to create atmosphere.

"I did a three-year apprenticeship in a small documentary film company before becoming a freelancer with my own equipment. In the future I'd like to move into the post-production area of sound editing, or mixing and preparing tracks for the last dub [the mixing of various layers of sound for the final soundtrack]."
Ray Beckett, sound recordist

Finally, the sound recordist has overall responsibility for the equipment and other members of the sound crew. It is important that the director thinks about the sound element of the film when looking at potential locations; highway or airport noise will drown out the actors' words, however good the equipment is.

The Sound Recordist

During pre-production, the main tasks of the sound recordist are to assemble the best possible team (including a boom operator and sound technician) and to check all the equipment. In the lead-up to production, the sound recordist discusses with the director how best to record dialogue and effects for each scene. He or she also contacts the people who will be doing the sound editing and mixing to see which recording equipment they prefer.

The sound recordist's first concern on set is to record as much usable dialogue as possible to be used in the finished film. His or her next task is to record background sound effects, especially those unique to a particular location or scene. Sometimes the sound recordist also has to record music played live on set. Once the shoot is over, he or she works with the editing team and records extra wild tracks if necessary to cover up any mistakes.

A sound recordist posing with booms. A boom is one of the sound recordist's most important pieces of equipment. It is held over the actors' heads to record dialogue, but the recordist must ensure that the boom is kept out of the shot.

Design

The production designer and art director will have brought together a team of set, costume, hair, and makeup designers who work throughout the production on their own specific areas. However, they must work closely with the director and DOP regarding questions of lighting and color, as any decisions of this kind may affect the film's "look" and need to be consistent with the director's overall vision.

Production management

To make sure the production stays on schedule and within budget, the producer and production manager or assistant produce daily "call" or schedule sheets and distribute them to all members of the cast and crew. These sheets detail the shooting schedule for the following day and include the scenes to be shot, the actors required, start times, contact numbers, transportation details, maps, and so on.

Continuity

The script supervisor or continuity person on set is responsible for making full and detailed notes on each

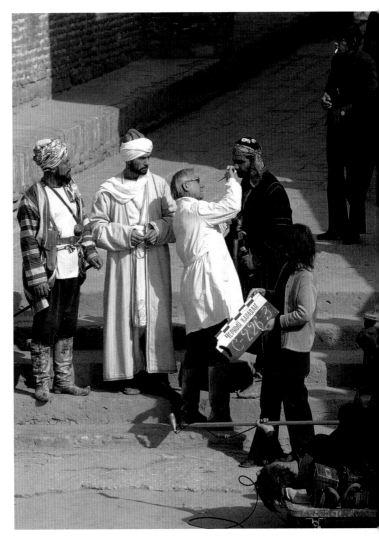

A member of the production design unit attends to an actor's makeup between shots.

The beginnings of continuity

Filmmakers quickly recognized that the way to keep the public interested was to show them a story that made sense in the way that the shots followed one another. By 1917, most of the basic continuity editing techniques had been established. They included intercutting (moving back and forth between actions in different locations) and contiguity editing (for example, when a character moves out of the frame and appears in a new place, moving in the same direction, in the next frame).

shot filmed to make sure that the content of the shot and scene match perfectly, even if they are not filmed on the same day. These notes should include the position of furniture and other props, the actors' exact words and gestures, and even such seemingly insignificant details as the length of ash on a burning cigarette.

One of the camera assistant's jobs is to clean the camera and keep it in good working order.

In addition, a "log" is kept. This is a document containing the technical decisions that are made each day during the making of a film. The camera assistant records the technical details of each shot filmed. The log is a vital part of the filmmaking process and is central to creative decision-making at all stages.

The rushes

At the end of each day, the images that have been shot are sent to a laboratory to be processed. From there they are returned to the set so that the director and DOP can look through them before starting again the next day. While viewing these "rushes," the director and DOP check for color, light, and sound quality, as well as continuity between scenes. Once they are satisfied, the rushes are sent to the editor, who starts to put a rough cut of the film together. Like the camera assistant

The director and some of the crew look at the rushes to see how the day's filming has turned out.

The camera operator working with the crew to set up a shot.

mentioned earlier, the editor's assistant keeps a log of decisions made in the cutting room. The "final wrap" means that all the scenes in the film have been shot (this is usually after about six weeks for a feature film). At long last, the cast and crew get a chance to relax at the mandatory "wrap party"!

JOB PROFILE

The Assistant Director

Organization, coordination, and the ability to communicate effectively are the main skills required of an assistant director. His or her job involves ensuring that everyone—the crew, the production office, and the actors—knows what is going on at all times during the production. The assistant director also recruits any extras (additional actors, usually hired for crowd scenes) that are needed and makes sure that the actors, in particular, know exactly when they should be on set. He or she works closely with the director and, along with the production office, attempts to solve any problems that arise from day to day.

The assistant director keeps order on set, plans each day's shooting with the director, and sets up each shot for the director's approval.

POST-PRODUCTION

In post-production, the pictures and sound are put together to create the final film. This stage involves fewer people than the production stage. These are mainly the editor, director, producer, special effects (SFX) experts, graphic artists, sound editors, and dubbing engineers. It also usually involves a composer, who provides an original soundtrack to accompany all or some of the images. The process starts with an editor's "rough assembly" of the film, produced immediately after or sometimes during the shoot. It ends with a "fine cut," which is when all the details of sound and image have been perfected according to the various requirements of the director, producer, and investors.

Until relatively recently, editing was a time-consuming process that involved the physical cutting and pasting (splicing) of pieces of film.

The editing process

In the past, editing a film involved literally cutting it up and putting the chosen shots together in a certain order. Now, most of this work is done by computer, which makes the process much faster and more flexible. If the director has chosen to shoot on film but wants to edit by computer, the film is first transferred onto videotape. This is known as the telecine process. The videotape is then fed into the computer system by way of a process called digitization. The editor selects the best shots and arranges them into sequences that convey a story and emotion.

Once the day's film rushes have been approved, they are transported to the post-production facility house, where they are viewed and logged by an assistant editor. This involves writing a short description of each shot to help make the editing process more efficient. If the telecine process is necessary, this will be completed, and the editor can form the rough assembly for the director and producer to discuss. This rough assembly gradually becomes a rough cut, then a fine cut or '"finished edit" when various decisions have been made. Digital technology gives the editor the chance to try out a number of different "mixes" of shots rather than coming up with just one. It also allows the editor to add things, events, or people that were never there during the shoot, such as huge crowd scenes, natural disasters, or "flying" actors.

Today, editors use computers to organize images and sound.

The sound

Sound editing is the process of adding the sound to the images, and assembling and mixing a range of sounds from different sources—music, dialogue, effects, and atmosphere—to form the film's final soundtrack. Sound editors follow a precise chart put together by the director. This acts as a road map, guiding them through all the sound requirements of the film. Elements such as the dialogue are "pre-mixed" to remove any unwanted extra noise from cameras, passing trucks, or aircraft, and to equalize the noise levels for all the actors' voices. If any dialogue needs to be re-recorded, the actors are called to a small studio to do this while watching the relevant piece of film. Once all the elements have been mixed together, the soundtrack, known as the "dub" or "final mix," is ready for the next stage.

The spread of political cinema

Beginning in 1930, groups of independent filmmakers around the world collaborated to make documentaries that recorded issues such as poverty and racism. However, the rise of fascism (a movement opposed to democracy and liberalism) and the start of World War II focused attention elsewhere, and by the 1940s this political movement had gone into decline.

Sound effects

The creation of sound special effects is the responsibility of specialist technicians called foley artists (after Jack Foley, the technician who invented the modern process of adding basic sound effects to action). These technicians can mimic certain sounds, particularly body movements, such as walking on a variety of surfaces, glasses being placed on a table, keys jingling, etc., and synchronize these with the actions on the screen. Foley artists have to be quite inventive, using a variety of props such as bells, whistles, and coconut shells, to make sure that no one notices their sounds are not real. Most dubbing studios also have massive effects libraries, which can be used to drop in sounds that were missed on set.

Soundtrack

Music adds atmosphere and emotion to a film and helps to create the overall feel. The composer may have been brought in to think about the original parts of the soundtrack at an early stage in filming. However, he or she usually prefers to start working on the soundtrack when the sound and image edits have been "locked off" and the editing process is complete. This way, the composition can be synchronized as closely as possible to the film. Today many composers work on computer, which makes the process more efficient; but real musicians are often brought in to play the music in a recording studio.

Final details

Editing is a long process, because every detail needs to be carefully checked and changed if a technical problem, such as a "drop out" (break in the sound), is found. Once the opening titles and credits have been added, the final step is

JOB PROFILE

The Composer

The composer's role is to compose, orchestrate, and conduct the music for the film, and oversee the score from the very beginning of composition to the final recording session. During pre-production, the composer reads the script and gets to know the story and characters well. Then he or she meets with the producer and director to discuss specific areas and general ideas for the music score. In some cases, he or she has to compose music for particular scenes where music is "featured"—for example, in a dance hall scene where the musicians are seen performing on stage.

The composer may attend filming when music is being used in scenes such as those just described, or simply to get a flavor of the film as it develops.

During post-production, the score is composed and preview sessions involving the music to be recorded take place with the director. Finally, the composer attends the dubbing sessions to help strike the right balance between the music, dialogue, and effects in the film.

Legendary composer Burt Bacharach at work on a film score.

usually the tape grade, when color is balanced out and contrast is added. Only when the investors and studio executives are totally satisfied with the quality and content will the film be considered "in the can."

Even then, the music supervisor will still be working on checking copyrights for any "borrowed" music used in the film, sorting out budgetary overspends, and delivering the final legal paperwork to the investors. Even a simple, well-known song such as "Happy Birthday" has to be paid for! Until this point, all post-production processes have been carried out on secondary material; the master is not touched until everything is in place. On final approval, the negative cutting can take place; this is the matching of the final edit to the master negative of the film. For an average feature film of 110 minutes with 800 cuts, this process can take an additional two weeks.

The conductor watches the action on screen to ensure that the mood of the music played matches that of the image as closely as possible.

Completion

Once the film is finished and approved, copies (prints) are made from the master negative. These will eventually be sent to theaters around the world. At this point, responsibility for the film is handed over to the distributor, whose job is to get people to know about the film and go and see it. If no distributor has yet made a commitment, the producer will take the film to festivals to try to stir up interest. But no big, expensive movie would be made without first having a distributor on board.

JOB PROFILE

The Editor

The editor's job involves putting together the pictures and sound recorded during the production stage of the film to tell a story in an understandable and entertaining way. At the same time, the editor needs to ensure that the emotional content of the film is consistent with the filmmakers' intentions. During pre-production, the editor looks at the storyboard for possible cutting problems; these might include shots that will need to be added in production to ensure the story makes sense. The editor helps the producer put together the post-production schedule so that enough time is allocated to the editing process. Then he or she will recommend a suitable (good and affordable) post-production suite where the editing and sound mixing can take place, and put together a post-production team, including sound editors, dubbing mixers, and graders.

While production is taking place, the editor sometimes advises on shots and how they will look together, but his or her main job is to put together the occasional rough cut of certain scenes for the director to look at while on set, or to try out visual effects experiments. In post-production, the editor oversees the whole process, keeping an eye on the sound editors, the labs, and production of titles and visual effects. He or she also produces the fine cut of the film in consultation with the director and with input from the producers and investors. When the film is complete, the editor is sometimes responsible for editing trailers (compilations of extracts used to advertise a film) and supplying clips (extracts) for publicity purposes.

Despite the introduction of new technology, editing can still take a long time. The increased possibilities for rearranging the footage mean that the director and editor have more options from which to choose.

THE JOURNEY TO THE THEATER

When the final cut of the film has been approved, it is shown to members of the distribution company, who will view it to discuss any changes that have been made. Then the distributors finalize their plans for managing the film's release.

Distribution

The distribution company's sales department is responsible for negotiating with the theaters. The print department makes copies of the film from the master and transports them to the theaters. The marketing department organizes the publicity so that people know the film is out, have an idea of what it is about, and are encouraged to spend their money on a ticket to see it. The distribution company's goal is to maximize box office potential so that the investors see a return on their money. In some cases, test screenings are organized for an invited audience, who are asked to comment on the film. On the strength of these comments, further changes may be made in the final edit to try to guarantee a positive public reaction. Usually, around 40 percent of the estimated box office earnings are spent on the print and advertising (P&A) budget.

Lining up to buy tickets at a box office in Barcelona, Spain.

The prints

Prints are the copies of the master that are sent out to theaters. These are very expensive, and it is important that the distributor accurately estimates the number of prints needed to satisfy all the likely requests to show the film. Because the distributor is experienced in dealing with similar films and has a knowledge of what sort of films do well in different locations, it is usually possible to reach an informed decision about the number of prints required. The distributor also has to decide when to release the film. This depends on a variety of factors, including the time of year, national holidays, likely competition from other films, relevance of the subject matter, and the dates of awards ceremonies such as the Academy Awards (Oscars). Some films are released in the months just before the Oscars. As such films are fresh in people's minds, the producers think they have a better chance of winning.

Winning an Oscar represents the highest achievement for many filmmakers and stars.

Sales

The distributor organizes a preview screening for the exhibitors, who are responsible for booking films into their theaters many months in advance. Bookings may well be made before the film is completed, as the exhibitors tend to make their decision based on information given and prior experience of the way in which similar films have performed at their theaters.

Media Fact

Changing to color

Although color filmmaking was introduced in the late 1930s with films such as *The Wizard of Oz* (1939), the use of color film as a popular medium did not become widespread until after World War II. Then it offered an appeal that television images of the day could not match.

Marketing

The marketing department coordinates the design and production of posters, trailers, and flyers and works on promotional tie-ins, merchandising, placing advertisements, and interacting with the press. It also works to generate word-of-mouth publicity by organizing preview screenings for invited audiences, who can be relied upon to tell their friends to see the film once it is released. If the film is good enough, some smaller productions with little to spend on a glossy marketing campaign may do very well simply through word-of-mouth publicity. On the other hand, the major distributors will spend millions of dollars marketing an expensive Hollywood blockbuster to make sure that it does well at the box office.

The marketing department may carry out audience research by inviting different types of people to watch the film and recording their reactions. This research gives the distributor an idea about the kind of audience to target and may help to kick off the word-of-mouth campaign.

Distributors recognize the importance of the free advertising that the press and broadcast media can provide. The marketing department puts together a press kit containing production notes, cast and crew credits, details of the stars, director, and producer, and a set of authorized photographs and sends it to print, TV, and radio journalists. A public relations company or specialist will often be employed to deal

Gala premieres of Hollywood blockbusters can attract huge media attention, particularly if attended by stars such as Sylvester Stallone.

specifically with this. If possible, interviews with the stars are arranged to give the film maximum publicity, and a special press screening is set up for all those preparing reviews in advance of the film's release. The release of a big-budget, high-profile film may be heralded by a gala premiere, with stars, celebrities, and media in attendance. At the premiere, guests may be asked for contributions towards a charity the film company has decided to support. This charity may be linked to the theme of the film or to something that one of the stars is involved with.

> "I see my work as documentary photography and enjoy trying to capture the feel and essence of a scene and the people involved with it. Each production is very different. What I don't like is all the hanging around on set waiting for my opportunity to take photos."
> *Marysia Lachowicz, stills photographer*

JOB PROFILE

The Stills Photographer

The role of the stills photographer is to keep a photographic record of the shoot. This includes taking photos of the crew as well as the actors. These photos are mainly used later on to produce flyers and posters to publicize the film. There are two types of film photography: unit stills, which involve spending lots of time on set photographing every scene as well as the actors and crew; and specials, for which the photographer is employed over a short period to set up specific shots for publicity purposes.

During pre-production, the stills photographer spends time with the director and producer discussing what type of shots they think they'll need and whether the photos should be in black-and-white or color. On set, he or she concentrates on capturing "behind the scenes" shots of the crew, photographing the action, and generally trying to recreate the essence of a scene in one photo. This involves the possibility of setting the shot up again after the filming has finished. The photographer then processes the films and delivers them to the production company or sales agent. If it is in their contracts, some stars have the right to see the photos and approve the way in which they are used. The production company then selects sets of photographs to use for publicity—to send to newspapers and to incorporate into posters and flyers.

The stills photographer works on set to record the production and set up shots for publicity purposes.

To maximize the potential for awareness and sales, the distributors of blockbuster films increasingly use merchandise and promotional tie-in campaigns. The production of toys, books, clothes, and school bags emblazoned with images from major films is now big business, as are video games that enable people to continue to experience the films and the characters in an interactive way. If the producers organize a tie-in with another large, well-known company (such as a burger chain), they can make greater profits for investment in merchandising.

Certification and ratings

In many countries, a film has to be given a certificate by the relevant government body before it can be screened to a paying audience. A video copy of the film is sent to the examiners, who give it a release certificate and rating. The examiners scrutinize the film for violence, bad language, and offensive behavior in particular. They may decide to cut a few scenes, or occasionally ban the film altogether. In the U.S., a voluntary rating system is run by the Motion Picture Association of America. The certificate or rating awarded the film affects the marketing campaign by giving the distributors a particular age group to target.

Cinema exhibition

At long last, the film reaches the theater, where it is hoped that people will pay to come and watch it. There are several different types of movie theaters—the multiplex, the traditional, the independent, and the art-house—and each tends to show a different type of film appealing to different audiences. In an independent theater, the manager makes the decision whether to show a film or not after careful bargaining with the distributor. For multiplexes, the director of the theater chain makes this decision. In each case, the theater managers work out how much an individual film is likely to "take" at the box office and whether screening it is worth the risk. Sometimes they have little choice: if the film is a Hollywood blockbuster with a huge marketing budget, it is much more likely to be shown at a multiplex than at an independent or art-house theater.

Theater building design has changed over the years to reflect fashions in architecture. The heyday of theater-going during the 1930s and 1940s saw a large number of neo-classical film theaters built in city centers.

Various activities take place at some theaters to attract the attention of the public. Educational and promotional programs, with practical workshops and guest speakers, may be targeted at young people to encourage them to try out different types of film.

In due course, most films are distributed in other ways to maximize box office potential for the investors. The films are transferred onto video and DVD and sold to cable and satellite movie channels for home viewing. Some films are never released in the theaters because the investors do not believe they will make enough money to cover the production and marketing costs. In most of these cases, the productions go straight to video.

GETTING A JOB IN THE INDUSTRY

"Get your hands on a video camera and some editing equipment and make your own short film—however basic and rough it seems to you. Film school is great if you can get there, but ideally you need some experience first."
Jean Stewart, director

These students are learning how to operate a camera and set up lighting in a studio.

There are many ways of getting into the film industry. One way is to get a degree in film studies and then go to film school; another is to work voluntarily as a production trainee. Most commonly, however, entry into the film industry involves a combination of the two.

The first step for those interested in becoming filmmakers is to watch different kinds of films to see how they are constructed. Go to the movies as much as possible, watch videos, and read scripts and filmmakers' biographies. Try to identify what it is you care most about and set

about giving it expression. While you are watching films, study how the different effects and emotions, such as tension, suspense, humor, and sadness, are produced. Then try your hand at making a short film of your own, however basic. It's fun, creative, and challenging, and it could be the beginning of the film career of your dreams.

Studying film

If you do get into college to study film, work to make contacts and learn as much as possible. Try to stay a step ahead of everyone else and put together an impressive resume. Use your contacts to try to gain experience on a film set, even if you start as a runner carrying out minor tasks to help the cast and crew.

If your ambition is to become a scriptwriter, the most important thing is to start writing! Comic books are a good discipline for writing for a visual medium. Don't aim too high too soon—it's important to get something made, even if it is just a four-minute script, so that the people you approach for funding know you are serious. You can also learn a lot about scriptwriting from watching the director and editor in action.

If your interest is in cinematography, start by looking at the effects of lighting in paintings, photos, and films. Observe how it changes the mood of an image. To become a sound recordist, you need to establish a good grasp of the theory behind sound; in other words, work hard at physics! Also try to establish a practical understanding of electronics and equipment maintenance. For cinematography and stills photography, you should study photography, in college or on your own time. For stills photography, you need to enjoy working with people and taking portraits of them. It is useful

"Live a little! Probably the most important thing for a writer is to have something else in your life—a partner, children, a religious faith, a political cause, a hobby—anything that can be at the center of your being so that it doesn't bother you too much when you get messed around."
Frank Cottrell-Boyce, screenwriter

Media Fact

The challenge of video and DVD

The recent prosperity enjoyed by the film industry is partly the result of new technologies, which provide new outlets for watching films. The first Betamax home video machine was introduced in 1975, and, by 1988, most U.S. households had a video recorder. After initial anxiety about possible competition, the film industry saw that showing films on video as well as in theaters was a real opportunity. By 1986, at least half the income earned by the major studios was from video sales. In the early 21st century, DVD offers yet another way of increasing a film's revenue.

to gain some experience by working on low or no budget films, so that you can put together a portfolio of your best work. Do your own research by looking at film magazines and finding out what sort of photos are most used to publicize different productions—then work along those lines.

A composer of film scores needs to gain a wide knowledge of all music styles—you may be composing a string quartet one day and a rock score the next! Develop good orchestration skills and an ability to produce music quickly and on deadlines. Develop musical direction skills—it is a huge asset if you can conduct your own music with confidence.

Casting for children's parts may involve setting up auditions in many areas and advertising at schools, community centers, and theater groups.

India has a highly successful and popular film industry known as "Bollywood." The film business is centered in the city of Bombay.

Hard work

If you do make it into the film business, the personal qualities you will need include persistence, vision, patience, determination to succeed, and excellent communication and problem-solving skills. Be prepared for long hours of hard, exhausting work, early starts, setbacks, and delays.

Above all, try to stick to your vision of how you want your film to look, regardless of any discouraging situations you might experience. Even the greatest filmmakers have suffered failure and disappointment on the road to success.

"Persistence is probably the most important quality to have, along with the obvious interest in film and its processes. Enthusiasm and a willingness to work long and hard for little or no reward also help—if you knock on enough doors, one of them will open for you. Most people I know who work in film started at the bottom and worked their way up. Specific jobs may require specific qualifications, but other than that I reckon anything goes!"
Luke Youngman, production assistant

"You should try to understand the purpose of everyone's job because it is such a team activity. You should also try and learn all about film history and look at how films in the past have been put together, how they build emotion and tell their stories."
Annie Kocur, editor

"Above all, follow your passion—you'll need a lot of that—and hang on in there! There's no traditional 'career structure,' no ladder to climb —but it could just all work out for you."
Jean Stewart, director

GLOSSARY

adaptation a film inspired by or based on a novel, play, article, TV series, or other source

blockbuster a big, expensive film, often made in wide-screen, lasting more than two hours, and usually an enormous box office success

boom from the Dutch word for tree, pole, or beam; a boom is a long pole with a microphone at one end

Cannes Film Festival the most prestigious film festival, held each May in southern France

censorship the act of deciding whether a film should be shown to the public

cinematography the operation of the camera, lights, stock, and lenses; it includes making decisions regarding color, composition, and camera movement and angles

clapperboard a small chalkboard with spaces for recording information, including the name of the film, director, date, and number of scene and take; the clapperboard is used to synchronize sound and image in post-production

continuity person a member of the production team who is responsible for making the film look as seamless and natural as possible

crane a mechanical, arm-like trolley used to move a camera through space above the ground

cut the editing method of connecting images, moving from one shot to the next

dubbing the process of adding sound to a film after it has been shot

DVD digital video disc; a medium for movies

exhibition the showing of a film to an audience in a theater

film stock film that has not yet been used to create images

footage the amount of film shot over a particular period, traditionally measured in feet

frame a still, rectangular, single image—the basic unit of film

genre a category of films that share common elements such as stylistic conventions, themes, plots, or character types; eg. horror, Western, science fiction

log the document used to record what technical decisions have been made during production and post-production

master the final copy of the completed film from which all further copies are made

rating the classification given a film to inform the public about the nature of its content

runner a junior production assistant employed to carry out minor tasks to help the cast and crew

rushes (also known as dailies) prints of each day's filming, viewed the following day by the director and director of photography to keep track of lighting and performance

shoot to film, or the process of filming

take a single run of film through the camera; several takes are made of the same shot until the director is satisfied with it

35mm the standard film width for commercial filmmaking

tie-in any cross-promotional activity, often in the form of offering free gifts to entice the public to see a new release

tracking shot a shot in which the camera moves on wheels, usually on specially laid tracks

trailer a short film advertising a forthcoming feature, made up of a compilation of clips and a voice-over

treatment a full description of a film's narrative, which should also give a sense of how the film might look

voice-over commentary on the film, either by one of the characters or by an unseen narrator

Western an action film set in the western states of North America, usually sometime between the end of the Civil War and the turn of the 20th century, featuring the exploits of cowboys and Native Americans

wide-screen a technique used to make the final film wider than usual on screen, often used for epic, action, or adventure films

wild track sound recorded separately from the images and added to the film for atmosphere

wrap the end of shooting of either a scene or a whole film

zoom a shot made with the use of a special lens that increases the size of the subject of the image (zoom in) or decreases it (zoom out)

USEFUL ADDRESSES

**Academy of Canadian Cinema &
Television**
http://www.academy.ca
172 King Street East
Toronto, ON M5A 1J3 Canada

**Academy of Motion Picture Arts and
Sciences**
http://www.oscars.org
8949 Wilshire Boulevard
Beverly Hills, CA 90211-1972

American Film Institute
http://www.AFI.com
2021 N. Western Avenue
Warner Communications Building
Los Angeles, CA 90027

Cannes Film Festival
http://www.festival-cannes.fr
3 rue Amélie F-75007
Paris, France

Dreamworks SKG
http://www.dreamworks.com
100 Universal Plaza #601
Universal City, CA 91608

Independent Feature Project
http://www.ifp.org
8750 Wilshire Boulevard, Second Floor
Beverly Hills, CA 90211

**John F. Kennedy Center for the
Performing Arts**
http://www.kennedy-center.org
Washington, DC 202566

Metro-Goldwyn-Mayer Studios
http://www.mgm.com
2500 Broadway Street
Santa Monica, CA 90404

Motion Picture Association of America
http://www.mpaa.org
15503 Ventura Blvd.
Encino, CA 91436

National Screen Institute
http://www.nsi-canada.ca
206, 70 Arthur Street
Winnipeg, Manitoba R3B 1G7 Canada

New York Film Academy
http://www.nyfa.com
100 East 17th Street
New York, NY 10003

Paramount Pictures
http://www.paramount.com
5555 Melrose Avenue
Los Angeles, CA 90038

Sony Pictures
http://www.sonypictures.com/movies
10202 West Washington Boulevard
Culver City, CA 90232

**Sundance Institute for Independent
Filmmaking**
http://institute.sundance.org
Box 3630
Salt Lake City, UT 84110-3630

Twentieth Century Fox
http://www.foxmovies.com
1211 Avenue of the Americas
New York, NY 10036

UCLA Theater, Film, and TV Studies
http://www.tft.ucla.edu
Box 951622
Los Angeles, CA 90095-1622

BOOKS TO READ

Begleiter, Marcie. *From Word to Image: Storyboarding and the Filmmaking Process*. Studio City, Calif.: Michael Wiese Productions, 2001.

Blandford, Steve. *The Film Studies Dictionary*. Oxford: Oxford University Press, 2001.

Bordwell, David, and Kristin Thompson. *Film Art: An Introduction*. New York: McGraw-Hill, 2001.

Bordwell, David, and Kristin Thompson. *Film History: An Introduction*. New York: McGraw-Hill, 1994.

Corey, Melinda. *American Film Institute Desk Reference*. New York: DK Publishing, 2002.

Goldman, William. *Adventures in the Screen Trade*. New York: Warner Books, 1989.

Jackson, Kevin. *The Language of Cinema*. New York: Routledge, 1998.

Jones, Chris, and Genevieve Jolliffe. *The Guerrilla Filmmakers' Handbook*. London: Cassell, 1999.

Lowenstein, Stephen. *My First Movie*. New York: Pantheon, 2001.

Mascelli, Joseph V. *The Five Cs of Cinematography*. Los Angeles: Silman-James Press, 1998.

Monaco, James. *How to Read a Film*. Oxford: Oxford University Press, 2000.

Parker, Philip. *The Art & Science of Screenwriting*. Bristol, UK: Intellect, 1999.

INDEX

Numbers in **bold** refer to illustrations.

Academy Awards (Oscars)
51, **51**
Adam, Ken 18
agents 22-23
Allen, Woody **12**
American Film Market 11
assistant director 43, **43**
Australian Film
Commission 10
Australian Film Institute 10

Bacharach, Burt **47**
best boy 36
"blockbuster" 41, 55
Bollywood **59**
boom operator **31**
box office 50, **50**, 52, 55

camera operators 30, **42**
Cannes Film Festival 11, **11**
casting 22, **58**
certification 54
child actors 23, **23**
clapper loader 34, **36**
composer 47, **47**
continuity 40
contracts 24
Culkin, Macaulay **23**

Depp, Johnny **22**
director 17, 20, 22, 25,
32-33, **32**, **33**
director of photography
(DOP) 34, 35, **35**, 42
distribution 48, 50-55

editing 44-46, **44**, **45**
editor 49, **49**

film premieres 23, **52**, 53
film school 56-57, **56**
film stock 25
film, types of
animation 4, **5**, 39
documentary 4, 5
feature 4-5, 26
"final cut" 33, 45
"final wrap" 42
foley artists 46

gaffer 36
Gibson, Mel **13**

Hitchcock, Alfred 17
Hollywood 4-5, **4**, 6, 9, 13

insurance 25
investors 10-13, 20

key grip 36

location
manager 26, 28
scouting 26
Lumiere, Auguste 4
Lumiere, Louis 4

marketing 52
merchandising 10, 54

pitching 6
post-production 44-49
producer 17, 20-21, **21**, 22
production accountant 20

production assistant 28, 29,
29, 39
production costs 7-11, 20

production designer 27, **27**,
39, **39**

"rough cut" 33, 45
"rushes" 41, **41**

screen tests 22
script
outline 9
treatment 9-10
script doctor 14
script editor 14
script meeting **14**
scripting 6, 10, 12-15
scriptwriter 13, **13**, 14-15, **15**
set dressers **28**
shooting 30-43
shooting schedule 19-20
shooting script 19
sound recordist 37-38, **37-38**
soundtrack 45-46, **48**
special effects 34, **34**
star system 31
stills photographer 53, **53**
storyboards 12, **16**, 17-19,
18-19
studio system 9

theaters 4, 54-55
Towne, Robert **13**
Truffaut, Francois 57

Westerns 5
wide-screen 52
"wild tracks" 37-38